Love Goes Both Ways

Surrendering to the Truth of Dependence

BILL, JILLIAN, AND JOREE HARBECK

WESTBOW*
PRESS
A DIVISION OF THOMAS NELSON
& ZONDERVAN

Cover Graphics and Author Photo compliments of Jim and Mary Whitmer Photography.

WestBow Press books may be ordered through booksellers or by contacting:

WestBow Press
A Division of Thomas Nelson & Zondervan
1663 Liberty Drive
Bloomington, IN 47403
www.westbowpress.com
1 (866) 928-1240

ISBN: 978-1-4908-3371-2 (sc)
ISBN: 978-1-4908-3373-6 (hc)
ISBN: 978-1-4908-3372-9 (e)

Library of Congress Control Number: 2014906605

Printed in the United States of America.

WestBow Press rev. date: 4/25/2014

Contents

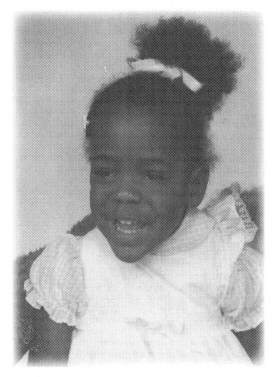

Joree, born January 17, 1991>

Introduction

Picture being confined to a wheelchair for every waking moment of your life. Imagine a physical disability that limits the freedom to command your body. Ponder the frustration of the inability to communicate with the world around you. Consider the limitations of living in this world physically challenged. We travel life's journey side by side, yet rarely do those blessed with health and strength engage with the wounded and broken.

Encountering people with severe disabilities is uncomfortable. We think, *What do I say? Do they understand me? Should I touch them?* Their appearance is unsettling; their mannerisms and uncommon behaviors stretch comfort zones. Yet we have natural feelings of empathy and compassion. There is an urge in every person's heart to reach out, even if just for a moment, to alleviate others' pain and suffering. We feel awkward, however, as we act politely, while hoping the time will pass quickly so that we can move back to the "real" world where life is "normal." These encounters, while rare for most of us in everyday life, may leave us feeling grateful and aware of our own blessings and good fortune. Or these encounters might pass by as just an uncomfortable anomaly of life.

Interacting with physically challenged people forces us to respond. Their disabilities are front and center. One can choose to ignore by walking on the other side of the street, or one can choose to be polite and courteous. But their visible maladies beckon a response. How we respond says a lot more about us than it does about our challenged neighbor. Interacting with the physically disabled is an opportunity for us to experience life in a unique way. It may be momentarily uncomfortable. However, those in wheelchairs or on crutches, those with Down's syndrome or autism, may, if we are willing, teach us more than any other experience about the beauty of life. If one intentionally engages in the world of the broken, the benefit is beyond measure.

While the world of physical disabilities is right in front of our eyes, what do we do with those among us who have wounded souls—something not as obvious? The woman walking past you on the street is being verbally and physically assaulted at home. How would you know? How could you recognize the adult survivor of sexual abuse? Could you imagine that the innocent child who is frolicking in the park is being molested at home?

Unlike physical disabilities, wounded souls are not easy to detect. While people with a hurting soul appear to be normal at first glance, a closer look reveals a host of disabilities. People with a damaged soul find it very difficult to communicate more than superficially. A level of trust and safety has been removed, so retreating to solitude and silence is safe. While managing social situations with proper decorum, those with hurting souls can be distant and aloof in close relationships. They often suffer in a silent world of loneliness and despair. They become entombed in toxic shame and guilt. Tragically, while these wounded walk among us, more often than not we fail even to see them. And so, unlike those with physical disabilities, these people with wounded souls frequently travel this world unrecognized, unsupported, and alone.

Physical disabilities and emotional disabilities, while vastly different in appearance, are quite similar in scope. The needs of those in the physically challenged community have become much better understood in the last few decades. Education and intervention have provided resources and acceptance of this deserving group. Unfortunately, understanding the nature of the wounded soul and how to respond lags far behind. If you are unfamiliar with both arenas, what you are about to read will help you understand the world of the broken. If you are challenged physically or emotionally, you will understand.

PART I

Living Life

CHAPTER 1

A Whole New World

It was January 17, 1991, and in the emergency room of a downtown Chicago hospital, a young mother had prematurely gone into labor. The nurses moved quickly, preparing all the items needed to care for a twenty-seven-week newborn. The lungs are not fully developed this early in a pregnancy, so the respiratory therapist set up oxygen equipment, anticipating breathing issues. Intravenous bags were readied for any necessary fluids, and an incubator was close at hand. Even after thirty-two weeks of gestation, life is risky for a newborn, but arriving at twenty-seven weeks instead of the usual forty could present numerous complications.

While preparing the mother for delivery, the nurses learned that she had a history of substance abuse. That was a probable explanation for the prematurity. They prepared for the additional trauma the baby might experience. There could be substance withdrawal symptoms or deformity. Even stillbirth was a possibility. The doctor hurried into the delivery room. The contractions became more intense.

"Bear down ... just one more push ... that's it. Good job, Mom!" The doctor smiled. "It's a girl." She was so little. Maybe three pounds. Complete. No visible deformities. She was gasping, and the nurses immediately attached her to the oxygen machines and the intravenous lines they had prepared.

The doctor examined the infant briefly and ordered the nurses to transport her to the neonatal intensive care unit as soon as she was stable. It took a couple of hours for her tiny body to adjust to the new, cruel world she had been thrust into. Once her vital signs were stable, the nurse rolled her down the hall in the incubator that was keeping her warm. She was in a very critical and precarious position, but the doctors and nurses were optimistic about her prognosis. They would monitor her every moment to be sure that she was receiving adequate oxygen and that her body temperature was consistent and stable.

The nurses transferred the mother to her own room and told her she would be able to get up in the morning to see the baby. For the time being, it would be best to get as much rest as possible. They told her that the prematurity was a big concern about the baby's future health, but as of that night, she was breathing (albeit with assistance) and her vital signs were stable and promising.

The nurses worked through the early morning hours to ensure the preemie was receiving the best care possible. Shortly after four o'clock in the morning, the alarms monitoring the newborn's breathing alerted the nurses to a problem. They quickly responded and recognized the baby was having severe seizures—not uncommon for premature newborns. The nurses increased the oxygen flow. Someone called for the delivery doctor and a neurosurgeon to report to the unit as quickly as possible.

The seizures lasted several minutes. The nurses watched with great concern as the doctors prescribed medications that would inhibit the tremors. Slowly the seizures stopped, but another episode followed an hour later. Finally, the visible signs of seizure ceased. However, there was a risk that additional seizures could occur. The nurses connected the baby's tiny body to another device to monitor minute seizure activity that could not be visually observed. Her vital signs were unstable, but her heart was strong. She was breathing properly, still with assistance from the machines. It was unknown if the seizures had done any damage to the brain. It would be days or even weeks before an adequate diagnosis could be determined.

Later that morning, the doctor examined the baby and met with the mother to inform her of the issues of the last six hours. He told her that the baby had suffered severe seizures during the early morning, most likely because of the prematurity. It was too early to know if the seizures caused any immediate damage. He cautioned her that seizures could continue, causing significant problems. He also mentioned that the baby was a beautiful girl.

"What would you like to name her?" the doctor asked.

The mother had two older children and was struggling to provide for them. She decided it would be best if she released the baby for adoption. She made the arrangements with the hospital and the Illinois Department of Children and Family Services, signed the paperwork, and left for home that afternoon. She chose not to see the baby before she left.

The precious little person was transferred to the high-risk care unit of the hospital. She was monitored around the clock for the first month. The health care system and the Department of Children and Family Services prepared for her care if she should ever leave the hospital. The seizures following birth had indeed been severe, and others had occurred in the weeks following. She had suffered a brain injury, which mandated that an emergency hydrocephalic shunt be inserted just under the skin of her scalp. Oxygen loss had resulted in severe cerebral palsy in all quadrants of her body. She would require intensive daily care in the days and months ahead, and her prognosis was guarded at best.

After three months, she was stable enough to be placed in a regular hospital nursery. The Department of Children and Family Services (DCFS) began the process of identifying a temporary placement for her for the time when she would be given the green light to leave the hospital. During her hospital stay, the nurses had decided to give her a name rather than to refer to her by the number assigned to her in the delivery room. They settled on the name Jeanine.

At five months old, Jeanine was a stable five-and-a-half pounds and was breathing safely on her own. She was unable to take a bottle, so she was fed by a nasogastric tube inserted into her nose to carry sustenance to her stomach. It was clear that the cerebral palsy had affected her entire body. Her mobility would be extremely limited. But Jeanine had an amazing smile, and all the caregivers in the hospital fell in love with her.

There are thousands of cases across the country like those of baby Jeanine—cases that require hours of medical and administrative effort by dozens of people to provide care for children with special needs. These dedicated workers are virtually unknown. They receive little if any attention in the public eye and garner little public appreciation for the heartfelt work they do for "the least of these."

On the morning of Jeanine's dismissal from the hospital, a DCFS worker packed up a few blankets, a couple pairs of pajamas, a package of diapers, as well as some formula and took Jeanine to a home that provided triage for children awaiting temporary placement in host homes. This was the home of Ms. Linda, as she was affectionately known. She was a licensed foster care parent who went above and beyond in her caring for newborns. Ms. Linda had the responsibility of her own three children and found time to love and care for four foster infants with special needs. The DCFS relied heavily on Ms. Linda, as unfortunately there are not many people willing to care for foster newborns—especially those with disabilities.

During this same period, Jillian, my wife, was ending a two-year recovery from a new health condition called chronic fatigue syndrome. Jillian had spent nearly all of those two years confined to home and bed. She was slowly regaining her strength. We discussed her going back to work and agreed that a couple days a week would be a good starting point. As fate would have it, Ms. Linda was in need of a part-time registered nurse to provide assistance with the medical issues of all the foster children in her care. She called Jillian, and they made plans to start the next week.

Jesus, here's another child to hold.
Keep this child safe and warm,
This world can be so cold.
Take this child in your arms,
And never let her go.
Jesus, here's another child to hold.

CHAPTER 2

Welcome Home

The front door swung open, and Jillian shouted, "Hey everyone, come and see what I have." The sound of dropping toys and shuffling feet came from the corners of the house, as children rushed to greet Mom in the living room. Jillian gently set down a basket and stood smiling from ear to ear, as the children peeked inside.

Looking puzzled, our oldest daughter, Jaimee, said, "It's a baby. Mom, what are you doing with a baby? Where's her mother?"

Jeff, the middle child, jumped in. "Why is that thing taped to her nose?"

"She's cute," laughed Julee, the youngest of the Harbeck children.

"I got her at work," Jillian responded.

"They're giving out babies at work?" Jaimee asked.

"Sort of," Jillian answered. "There were six there today, and the DCFS only allows a house to have five. Since it's Friday, one would have had to go back to the hospital. They decided a caregiver who was a registered nurse could bring one home for the weekend. I thought it would be fun to bring one home, so I did. Her smile is absolutely precious."

"What's her name?" asked Jaimee.

"Jamie," answered Jillian.

"Oh boy, that's not going to work."

"What will Dad say?" Julee asked, smiling.

"He'll be fine with it," Jillian responded. "She's only staying for the weekend. I'll take her back on Monday, and most likely DCFS will have a permanent place for her next weekend."

"So what's the thing in her nose, Mom?" Jeff repeated.

"It's how we feed her."

"You're kidding, right? What's wrong with a bottle, like normal kids?"

"Well, she's not a normal kid."

"She looks pretty normal to me. What's wrong with her?"

"It's a long story that I can share with you at dinner tonight. Right now, I need to clean the feeding tube before I feed her. You might not want to watch this; it looks kind of scary pulling the tube out of her nose."

"Cool," Jeff said. "I'll watch."

"Of course," Jaimee quipped. "Boys never have a problem with the gross stuff."

"How about you, Jaimee," Jillian asked. "Do you want to see me pull the tube out?"

"Will it hurt her? I don't want to watch if it hurts her."

"I'm sure it's a little uncomfortable, but I don't think it hurts. We wouldn't be doing it if it really hurt her."

"Okay, I'll try," Jaimee responded cautiously. Jaimee was fourteen years old at the time and always skittish about medical issues. Blood had a way of giving her dizzy spells. Getting her tonsils out had rivaled open-heart surgery in her mind, and the idea of pulling a fourteen-inch-long tube out of a baby's nose was a little scary.

"C'mon, Jaimee," teased Jeff. "You're such a wimp." Jeff, two years younger than Jaimee, was a self-confident young man without any reservations about blood and guts.

"How about you, Julee?" Jillian asked.

"Okay." Julee, only seven years old and not quite sure what was going to happen, sided with her tough brother.

"All right then, here goes," Jillian announced. She grasped the end of the flexible tube protruding from the baby's nose. With one quick motion, she tugged on the tube. It seemed like it would never end. The baby flinched and gasped a little as the tube came out.

Jaimee jumped up, moaned, and headed for the other room. Julee just sat, a little startled. Of course Jeff let out the expected, "Ahhhh, that was coooool."

The baby wiggled her nose and blinked a little, then gave everyone a big smile. It certainly didn't seem to bother her too much.

"Why do you have to do that, Mom?" asked Julee.

"It's the only way we can feed her right now. The tube goes through her nose, down her throat, and into her stomach. I attach a syringe to the tube and we pour the milk right into her stomach."

Still not sure, Julee asked, "Are you sure it doesn't hurt her?"

"I'm sure, Julee," Jillian responded with a smile.

"It's a good thing that you are a nurse. It makes it easier doesn't it?"

Jeff had already headed outside, knowing all the gory stuff was over. Jaimee came back in the room, asking, "Are you done yet, Mom?"

"Yes, Jaimee, and there is blood all over the place. It's a mess … just kidding."

Jaimee sat down next to Jillian and the baby. "How long is she going to stay with us, Mom? Why can't she take a bottle like other babies? Who does she belong to? What's her name?"

Jillian responded, "How about I get a salad made to go with dinner and we can talk about it then." She headed off to the kitchen, leaving Jaimee and Julee to watch over the evening surprise.

I was working as a carpenter at the time and usually didn't arrive home from work until after six o'clock in the evening. I remember walking in the house thinking, *Yes, it's Friday. Pizza night. Maybe play some catch with Jeff before it gets dark, and then relax a little, since I can sleep in tomorrow.*

Julee met me at the door with a goofy look on her face. The kind that makes you wonder what they're up to. "Hi, Dad," she said, smiling.

"Hi, Julee," I responded." She just stood there, smiling that goofy grin. Moments passed. Finally, I said, "So, what's going on?"

"Nothing."

"What's with the smile?" I asked.

"Mom has a surprise for you."

Great, I thought. Surprises usually were either very expensive or had a lot of work attached to them. I was guessing that since it was June, I wasn't going to be sleeping late tomorrow.

"Really, what kind of surprise, Julee?"

"Guess."

"A new motorcycle?"

"Daaaad," she said with a perturbed look. "Really ... guess."

"I have no idea, Julee."

Just then, Jeff walked through the door and said, "Hi, Dad. Have you seen Mom's new baby?" I have to admit that for just a second I was frozen. *Baby ... baby?* How could that be? She had a hysterectomy four years earlier. So that was not possible. A few other scenarios ran through my mind quickly as Jillian came into the room smiling.

"The kids told you, didn't they?"

"Sort of," I responded. Jillian is a remarkable woman. She epitomizes winsomeness. Forever smiling, forever the positive person and influence in the room. Nothing ever seems to rattle her, and even if it does, it is not for long. Therefore, when she said she brought a baby home from work, I wasn't very surprised. I assumed she would have a good reason and would convince all of us that it would be good for the baby, and us too.

I ordered the usual Little Caesar's Friday pizza, and we all sat down with the new bundle of joy. We had not had a baby in the house for some seven years. She was awfully cute, and she didn't fuss much at all. The kids explained the tube removal incident they had witnessed earlier, and Jeff was sure to make it as graphic as possible.

"Mom, you said you would tell us why you have to feed her with a tube," said Julee.

I was aware that Jillian was working for a friend in town who was caring for children with special needs, so I was not caught off guard by Julee's comment. There was a lot of excitement around the dinner table that night. It wasn't the kind of thing that happens very often. Maybe a lost puppy sometime, but this was a baby. Thus, we were all intrigued by her and were eager to hear the details. We finished the pizza, while Jillian related to us the little girl's story.

"She is six months old. She was born in Chicago prematurely with breathing difficulties and had seizures not long after she was born."

"What are seizures?" Julee asked.

Jillian explained that seizures are little spasms that can occur in the body or in the brain. In this case, the seizures were in the brain. When the seizures happen, oxygen doesn't get to the brain. When oxygen isn't there, it damages the area where the oxygen has been stopped. The longer the brain goes without oxygen the more damage is done to the brain. In this case, they feared that this infant had been without oxygen for quite a long time and that the damage was bad. They had diagnosed cerebral palsy. They were fairly sure it was in her arms and legs, meaning she wouldn't be able to walk.

"Is that why you have to feed her with the tube?" Jaimee asked.

"Exactly. She hasn't learned how to take a bottle, and it is hard for her to swallow without choking. So, for now she has to be fed with the tube. The doctors aren't sure if she will learn that or not," Jillian said. "There are a lot of things they are not sure about for her future. Walking, talking, eating—all of those won't be known until she grows older. There is also a chance that she will get sick a lot. She can get pneumonia or infections, and some doctors think she may not live long because of that."

Julee was sitting next to the baby and trying to get her to laugh. Julee looked over to Jillian and asked, "So, what are we going to call her? We can't have two Jaimees."

"Well, it is a little complicated right now," Jillian answered. "The day after she was born, her mother decided to give her up for adoption."

"Why?" asked Jeff.

"Well, her mother had other children, and when she heard that the baby had some serious physical problems and they may be for her life, she decided that she would not be able to care for her. It would be better to let someone else care for her."

"That must have been a hard choice," Jaimee said.

"Her mother didn't give her a name, and so the nurses in the hospital started to call her Jeanine. Her birth certificate says Jeanine. She has been in the hospital since she was born, and for some reason someone started calling her Jamie. They call her that at the house where I am working."

I chirped in at that point. "Jeanine, Jamie, little baby, whatever—she is only going to be with us for a weekend, so let's just stick with Jamie."

"What is going to happen to her, Mom?" asked Jeff.

"I don't know, Jeff. For now, she is going to stay here in town with the other children until the state agency can find a home that wants her."

"Why don't we take her?" Jeff said excitedly.

Big smiles of approval came to Jaimee and Julee instantly. Jillian deflected the idea quickly as she glanced at me and saw the look of consternation on my face. "I'm not sure that is something we can do right now, kids," Jillian said. "She has a lot of real needs and we already have three children. Her care will probably require a lot of time and energy. She is not going to be like other children. Besides, they will find a place for her very soon."

"What if they don't?" Jeff responded.

"That's not really for us to worry about right now," I said. "A home has to have a special license to be able to do that, and we don't have one, so we couldn't do it anyway."

With that rather deflating comment, we finished dinner. Julee asked if she could take little Jamie to watch TV with her. "Sure," Jillian said, "let me clean up here. Then I will come in and we can feed her while you are watching TV."

She was very little. Not much bigger than Julee's dolls. Little Jamie had a delightful personality. She rarely cried or fussed, and she didn't show any signs of disability. She was a little floppy when you picked her up, but this didn't seem to be very different from any other baby her age.

After the kids were in bed, Jillian and I talked for quite a while about the home where little Jamie was staying and the circumstances that brought her to us for the weekend. I heard more information that she hadn't shared with the kids. Little Jamie had already shown signs of future problems. Her susceptibility to pneumonia was a big concern, and the doctors told the caregivers it might take her life before she turned two. Her life expectancy without closely guarded care could be short.

If the cerebral palsy (CP) were as extensive as they predicted, she would face a series of developmental issues. The spasticity of CP would confine her to a wheelchair her entire life. That meant she would require twenty-four-hour total care.

As Jillian and I discussed and pondered her future, we touched lightly on what it would mean for our family if we were ever to consider fostering. There were licenses to apply for. What would it cost? Could we adapt our home to meet the needs? How would it affect our children? We certainly didn't want to take away our commitment to their well-being.

We concluded that it would definitely make a difference in our family's development. It would have a significant impact on the children and us. We were not in the position to handle anything like it. Our emotions about the baby were clear (she won you over in an instant), and the idea of someone not caring for her spoke to our hearts. On that weekend, however, it seemed clear that this was not a course we could pursue. So, we thought, let's enjoy the weekend with her and love her like our own in the little time we have with her. Monday she would go back with Jillian, and we would be better for the experience.

Monday came, and after the kids left for school, Jillian packed up little Jamie and headed to work. It had been quite a weekend. The novelty of the experience had created in all of us a sense of joy and fulfillment. The kids doted over her constantly and were so excited to show her off at church on Sunday as their new family friend. It was hard for us to say goodbye, but it had been a delightful three days.

When Jillian went to work the next Thursday, the home was once again faced with the overcrowding issue. Since we were not licensed, it was pushing the line a bit to have the baby with us again, but the only other option was someone from DCFS coming all the way out from Chicago and then returning on Monday. Jillian offered again for the weekend, and Friday afternoon when we all came home, to our delight, little Jamie greeted us again. The kids were thrilled, and although I was reluctant to admit it, I too believed it was good to have her back with us.

That weekend Jillian and I discussed the situation at the group home and the difficulty of caring adequately for so many special needs kids. We pondered the idea of securing a temporary foster care license that would allow us to keep little Jamie on weekends or for extended periods if necessary. On Monday, Jillian explored with the caregivers what was involved in getting a foster care license. They said that there would be extensive paperwork, fingerprinting, and home inspection. If everything met the state requirements, even a quick process would take about six to nine weeks to receive the license.

We presented the proposal to the children. Deciding was a nobrainer. The kids were thrilled with the idea. Jaimee and Julee debated over whose room she would stay in. We talked about hauling the crib out of storage and began preparing for another baby in the house.

We contacted DCFS, assuming that we were starting a process of at least six weeks. For reasons unknown to us, only seven days after little Jamie's first visit with us, the DCFS representative informed us that we had a temporary license and could begin taking children immediately. That was unheard of in the DCFS bureaucratic structure. So, without missing a beat, little Jamie returned for a second and third weekend in a row, and we agreed to keep her until DCFS could find a permanent placement.

It didn't take long to establish a new routine. Little Jamie, almost eight months old, was still being fed with a nasogastric tube. She had not learned to take a bottle and was unable to support herself in any way. Yet, with her smiles and giggles, she stole your heart every time you looked at her. It only took Jillian about three weeks to teach Jamie to take a bottle. She slept quietly through the night. Within a month or so, she had become just another member of the family. Little Jamie had a new home.

The only unresolved issue seemed to be that we had two children with the same name. So, once again we gathered as a family to discuss another name for little Jamie. Jillian had just one rule: the new name must start with the letter J, as the names of all of our other kids did. This would be only fair to our new baby. The discussion began, and several names were bandied about. After a brief debate, the name Joree was unanimously chosen—another J in the family.

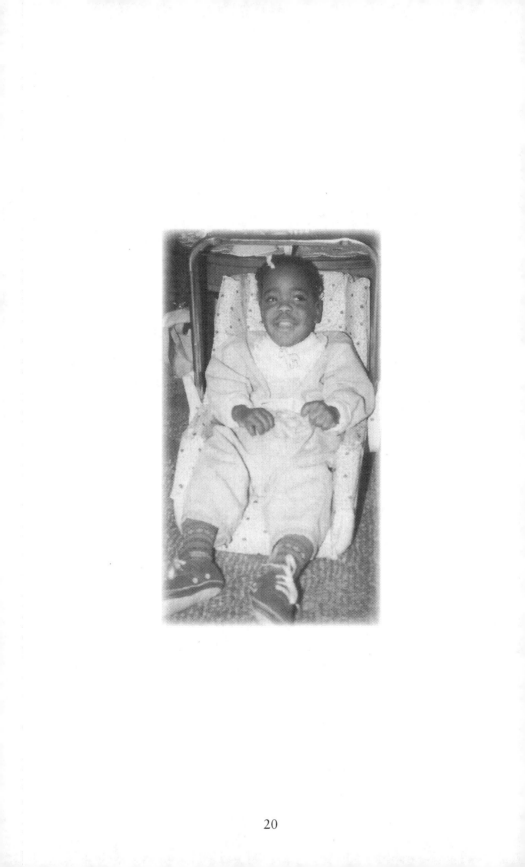

CHAPTER 3

"They're Gonna Have to Go through Us to Get Her"

Choosing a name is easy. Adapting to a new baby, though, is always a challenge for a family. In this case, adjusting to a child with special needs added some new challenges. The first year, there were not any major changes. It was the time Joree slowly became a part of the family and our extended family. We welcomed her with open hearts and arms. After three years of foster care, it was as if she had always been with us.

As Joree grew, however, the physical challenges we knew were there began to emerge. Eating was a difficult chore. Learning to drink from a cup and to swallow solid food was a slow process.

Because of the cerebral palsy, she had no stability in her limbs or back, so she could not support herself. Adaptive chairs, car seats, bath chairs, and strollers were required for transport and daily functions. She needed diapering.

An ability to speak was something we desired so much for her to experience. As the years began to roll past, however, it became clear that her disabilities would be more profound than we had imagined. Yet, even in her early development, there was always the smile, the giggling, the joy. Joree has always been about joy.

The first four years of relative ease in care gave way to the increasing awareness of the limitations Joree would have and the adjustments we as a family were going to make in the process. Joree was susceptible to respiratory ailments. Her spasticity meant that as she developed, her limbs and back would be compromised by the ever-pulling muscles on her skeleton. Eating became more and more a challenge and a lengthy process. Usually, children develop and grow; they understand and adapt. Joree was gaining weight and developing motor skills very slowly, and our role as a family of caregivers became very clear.

In those first four years, we did not dwell much on the changes the situation required of us. We adapted with Joree, and she grew into our hearts, despite all the challenges and her inability to communicate any ideas or thoughts at that stage. On several occasions, the DCFS visited us and requested that we move quickly toward adoption. One time they called and informed us that they were coming by that afternoon to pick up Joree, as they wanted to move the process along and felt they had a plan for doing so. They never showed up. It was the third such call that prompted the experience I describe in the following paragraphs.

I got home at the usual time this particular day and reached to open the back door, only to find it locked. Jillian's car was in the driveway, so that meant she was home. We never locked the back door, even when we went out somewhere. (Our community, Wheaton, was very safe.) It was peculiar, so I knocked to see if anyone was within hearing. No answer. I walked to the front door and it too was locked. I knocked, and I looked in the window but saw nothing. All was quiet. *Strange*, I thought. I walked around the house and still didn't hear anyone. The kids must be at their friends, I surmised, and maybe Jillian was next door.

I walked back around to the side door, and I heard the handle turn slowly. The door creaked as I gently pushed it open. A boy's voice softly said, "Dad, is that you?"

"Yes, Jeff. Why are you whispering? What's going on? Where's Mom?"

The door opened quickly. "Hurry up, Dad," he said. "Get in here."

I hustled inside, and Jeff quickly closed and locked the door behind me. In his hand was a baseball bat, and he looked concerned.

"What's happening?" I asked. "Is everyone alright?"

"For now," he said.

Julee emerged from the other room wearing a helmet and carrying a plastic sword. They had my attention. They escorted me to the front door, where they had piled chairs, toys, and pillows to keep the door from opening. They had done the same at the other exits. They were waiting for me before continuing their barricading.

"Are we expecting an invasion?" I asked.

"You're not going to believe this, Dad. DCFS called again, and they said they will be here in two hours to take Joree. Julee and I have everything in front of the doors so they can't get in."

"They're gonna to have to go through us to get her," Julee said with a determined look that brimmed with confidence.

Jillian came in from the other room, smiling. "Did they tell you?" she asked.

"They did. What's this all about?"

"Well, DCFS called again, and this time they say they are serious," Jillian explained. "Since we haven't agreed to adopt Joree, they are coming to get her and will place her in a family ASAP. They are concerned we are not committed to her and that as she grows she will not be exposed to her own culture and that it will only exacerbate her disabilities. You can see how the kids feel."

How many times are we going to go through this? I thought. It was time to call their bluff. I told the children to go to the garage and get me a broom I could use to help defend the homestead from the invaders. First, though, I would call DCFS and let them have a piece of my mind.

"This has gone on long enough," I declared forcefully, as I prepared to make the call.

"Right on, Dad. You show 'em," said Jeff and Julee, as they left to find a broom.

After four transfers, I was finally connected with the person at DCFS who could address my concerns. "I understand you are once again planning to come to our home to take Joree," I said.

"Ma'am, with all due respect, this is the fourth time this has happened, and each time no one shows up to follow through. You are creating a lot of stress and emotional pain for our family. I understand your desire to see Joree adopted, but this constant pressure by threatening to take her is enough."

I continued. "If you have a home that is ready to accept her today with all of her disabilities and special needs, then I will drive her to you this afternoon. If not, then would you please leave her and us alone? We will continue to consider adopting her when you eliminate the threats. Thank you very much."

When the call was over, a triumphant Jeff said, "Attaway, Dad. You told her."

"Would you really take her to them, Dad?" asked Julee hesitantly.

"Julee," I said, "I don't really believe they will find someone that will want her. I think she belongs here with us. Don't you?"

"Yeah, I do."

We did not hear from DCFS again.

Bill, Jillian, and Joree Harbeck

Heaven's Very Special Child

A meeting was held quite far from earth.
"It's time again for another birth,"
Said the angels to the Lord Above.
"This special child will need much love."
Her progress may seem very slow.
Accomplishments she may not show,
And she'll require extra care
From the folks she meets down there.
She may not run or laugh or play.
Her thoughts may seem quite far away.
In many ways she won't adapt
And she'll be known as handicapped.

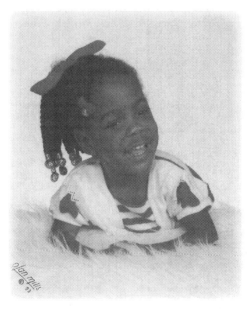

So let's be careful where she is sent.
We want her life to be content.
Please, Lord, find the parents who
Will do a special job for you.
They will not realize right away
The leading role they're asked to play.
But with this special child sent from above
Comes stronger faith and richer love.
And soon they'll know the privileges given
In caring for their gift from heaven.
Their precious charge, so meek and mild,
Is Heaven's very special child.
—Author Unknown

CHAPTER 4

Joree and the Angels

"Dad ... Dad ... Wake up!"

"Jeff, it's three in the morning. What's going on?"

"Dad ... the angels are here again. You gotta hear this."

Angels? I thought. *This ought to be good.*

I reluctantly pulled myself out of the warm bed and quietly followed Jeff down the hall, trying not to disturb the others. Jeff put his finger to his mouth. "Shhh," he whispered. "Don't let her know we are here."

It was very quiet for a few moments. Then we heard a soft, sweet little giggle. It came again a moment later. Suddenly, there was a burst of laughter, and Jeff and I covered our mouths to keep Joree from hearing us snickering.

"See, Dad, I told you. Every night the angels come to talk to her." The giggling and laughing continued for the next ten minutes without any indication of its cause. Each time, it was so entertaining that Jeff and I could not resist laughing along. After ten minutes or so I whispered, "You better get to bed, Jeff—6:00 a.m. comes really fast ... Good night, son."

Jeff was still giggling as he headed back to bed. "Good night, Dad."

I crept back to my room, thinking, *Angels—that's cute. The kids have such a wonderful imagination.*

I was still smiling as I crawled back in bed, and I began to ponder a bit. *You don't suppose there really could be angels? I mean, there was no one in her room; there was no other sound ... Naw, I don't think so,* I concluded, as I drifted back to sleep.

The next morning, I walked into the kitchen, where Jillian and the kids were already eating breakfast. I grabbed the cereal box, and Jillian asked, "What was going on last night? I heard you get up."

Jeff caught my eye and tried not to laugh. "Jeff, why don't you tell Mom what happened," I prompted.

"Joree's angels were back," Jeff replied matter-of-factly.

"You're goofy, Jeff," said Jaimee.

"No, it's true, Jaimee. I heard them too," Julee chimed in. "They come every night."

"Right. How do their wings get through the closed windows?" said Jaimee, a bit sarcastically.

"Jaimee, really. Angels are spirits; they don't have wings. They talk to your soul," Jeff informed us.

"You can believe whatever you want; I don't think it's angels," responded Jaimee.

I jumped in. "I heard it too, Jaimee. I have to say, it was really cute and funny—and there was no one touching or talking to her. I kind of lean toward the angel thing too."

"Told you," Jeff quipped to Jaimee.

"I hear her every night too; I just don't think there are angels in our house, that's all," Jaimee stated with certainty.

Jillian had gone to get Joree, and she came back into the kitchen with Joree in her arms, just catching the end of Jaimee's last statement. Jillian asked, "There were angels in your room last night?"

"Not my room."

"Yeah." Jeff jumped in. "Dad and I listened outside Joree's door. Every night she starts giggling like someone is tickling her. It lasts for like thirty minutes, and then she goes back to sleep. Jaimee doesn't think it's angels. She thinks Joree just wakes up for no reason and starts laughing."

"What do you think, Julee?" asked Jillian.

"I think it's funny. She makes me laugh."

Jaimee attempted to defend her position. "I think it is funny too. I just don't believe it is angels, that's all."

"So what do you think, Bill?" Jillian asked with a smirky smile.

"Well, I heard her myself, and I understand Jeff's point about the angels, and I agree with Julee that it is very funny, and I recognize Jaimee's point that we don't encounter angels much in this life, so ..."

"Forever the diplomat—aren't you, honey?" said Jillian, with a gentle smile.

"Well, I do know this," I said. "That little girl is filled with joy. I hope it just keeps rubbing off on all of us."

I believe there are Angels among us
Sent down to us from somewhere up above
They come to you and me, in our darkest hours
To show us how to live ... to teach us how to give
And guide us with a light of love.

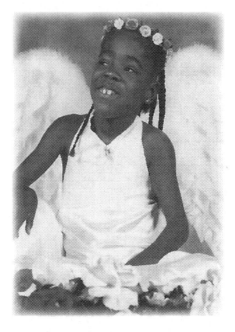

When life held troubled times and had me down on my knees
There's always been someone to come along and comfort me
A kind word from a stranger to lend a helping hand
A phone call from a friend to just say, I understand
Now ain't it kind of funny at the dark end of the road
Someone lights the way with just a single ray of hope
They wear so many faces
Show up in the strangest places
Grace us with their mercy
In our time of need
I believe there are Angels among us
Sent down to us from somewhere up above
They come to you and me, in our darkest hours
To show us how to live ... to teach us how to give
And guide us with a light of love.
—"Angels among Us," lyrics by Don Goodman and Becky Hobbs

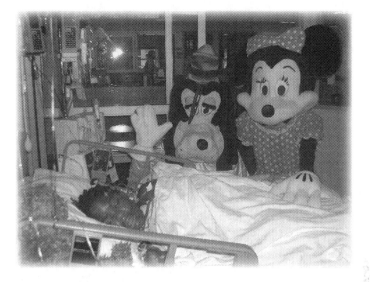

CHAPTER 5

No Stranger to Hospitals

In 1998, I accepted a position at Northwest Christian School in Phoenix, Arizona. Jaimee by this time was married, and Jeff was starting college. After a lifetime in Illinois, we picked up and moved with Julee and Joree to a new place, to make a new start.

At this juncture, Joree was seven years old, and her conditions were causing what the doctors had predicted would occur as she developed. Her spasticity was causing her bone structure to be compromised. This in turn would affect her internal organs, specifically causing malfunctions of digestion. She also was not eating well and was losing weight. Thus, the doctors determined that a "button"—a permanent gastric feeding tube—should be surgically inserted into her abdomen to provide for regular and efficient feeding. The next ten years saw a major surgery every year, each with a minimum seven-day hospital stay. One of the experiences of checking her in for surgery went as follows:

A receptionist at the hospital asked me, "What is Joree's birth date?"

"January seventeenth, 1991," I responded.

"Is she allergic to any medications that you know of?"

"No. She is on a couple of permanent meds, including phenobarbital, to manage and prevent seizures. She has not had any noticeable seizures for over ten years now."

"So, would you say that Joree is in good health?"

That question stopped me for a moment. The receptionist was efficiently gathering the information she needed to register Joree for the scheduled surgery. The receptionist had no idea what that question meant for Joree and us in the big picture. Joree had endured nine major surgeries over the preceding eight years. Two of them were especially significant, requiring sixteen-day hospital stays. The second of these operations involved the removal of eight feet of Joree's small intestines. A serious blockage had threatened to destroy her with serious infection. In both cases, Jillian and I were with Joree around the clock through the stays. Joree's basic inability to communicate with words makes it very difficult to understand her when she is simply moaning. Knowing her as we do, we are able to distinguish between moans that signify pain and moans that represent boredom or frustration. Remembering those long and tedious hours reminded me again of the pain and helpless feelings we endured for hours as she recovered.

"Mr. Harbeck ... Excuse me, Mr. Harbeck." The receptionist's voice snapped me out of my pondering.

"Yes, I am sorry. What was your question?" I said.

"What brings Joree here today?"

"She is scheduled for spine surgery with Dr. White," I replied.

The receptionist completed the paperwork and handed me a wristband to serve as Joree's identification during her stay. Beside Jillian and me sat Joree, vocalizing to her music, as her tape player filled the lobby with her favorite tunes. She was her usual cheery self, unaware of the next adventure in the children's hospital that was unfolding.

A nurse greeted us and wrapped a bright pink bracelet on Joree's wrist. We headed off to the surgery department. This was going to be a complicated and extensive surgery to place a fourteen-inch rod along her spine. The scoliosis of Joree's spine, caused by her extreme spasticity, was beginning to compromise her vital internal organs.

Three months earlier, Dr. White had counseled us that if we declined the surgery, the scoliosis would worsen, eventually crushing Joree's organs and bringing about her demise. The surgery would provide her a better quality of life. Dr. White had performed this surgery successfully on hundreds of other patients. We inquired about any alternatives. Ultimately, the surgery was a no-brainer for us; we were convinced this was best for Joree. We told Dr. White to go ahead at his convenience.

"Why is it always so cold in these rooms?" Jillian said half jokingly.

"Hospital policies," responded a nurse. "We will get Joree changed and then get her a nice warm blanket while she is waiting."

Doctors and nurses began surgery preparations as Jillian changed Joree into her hospital gown. The anesthesiologist stopped in to review with us the timeline for the surgery. He assured us that he would monitor all of her vital signs and pain management during the surgery and recovery. The nurse gave Joree a sedative to relax her before the surgery.

A short time later, Dr. White stopped to visit us and explain the procedure from his viewpoint. He walked us through each step. The operation should take four or five hours. He would initiate an incision along the entire length of her spine. Two screws would be anchored in her pelvis. The rod would be wired to every other vertebra along the spine from her neck down.

After surgery, Joree would have to be up in her wheelchair an hour after she was in her room, to assure the rod was placed correctly and to alleviate any fluid buildup in her lungs. He told us he would do his best to keep her as comfortable as possible. Dr. White is a master surgeon, but even better, his heart for Joree and our well-being set us at ease that day. He shook our hands, spoke briefly with Joree, and let us know that as soon as he was finished, he would be out to report on her condition.

The medication was taking effect. Joree's eyes were heavy; her arms and legs began to release their typical tightness. The nurse came in and checked her IV and vital signs. "Okay, time to go," she announced.

We gathered Joree's things, piled them on her wheelchair, and walked alongside the bed as the nurses wheeled her toward surgery. We had been through this routine many times. As we approached the door where we would part, Jillian and I again reflected on this moment. We have resolved ourselves to the truth that one of these times, Joree will not come home with us. That all the years of pain and suffering will be over for her. That we will have to let her go. However, at this time we were trusting in our Lord and in Dr. White's expertise. We leaned down, kissed Joree's cheek, and told her we loved her. Without hesitation, she responded to our kisses the way she always does—a big, wonderful smile. Her eyes twinkled, and if she could have spoken, I believe she would have said, "Don't worry, guys. I'll be just fine."

The doors closed behind her. The familiar feeling of helplessness returned as we made our way to the waiting room. Jillian and I offered up a prayer for Joree and Dr. White. We settled in for the long wait.

There are some in our world that argue Joree's surgeries are unnecessary. The expense to correct her disabilities only emphasizes the burden on our health system. They contend that children with severe disabilities and little function should be allowed to let life take its normal course. Prenatal decisions should be made for the better of the whole, and children like Joree should be aborted. She can make no valuable contribution to the good of others, and she is a drain on resources that could be used for those children that will produce.

Sitting in the waiting room, I wrestled with those ideas. This was Joree's ninth surgery. There was never a prognosis that suggested that one day she would walk and talk. She is confined to her wheelchair. She is fed through a gastric tube. She requires twenty-four-hour care. Some might ask, What possible benefit is she to this world? Why keep fixing an unfixable problem? In some circles of thought, I would hear the comment, "If there is a God, and he is a God of love, why does he allow this to happen?"

Feeling frustrated and anxious with my thoughts, I also reflected on what I experienced from Joree's surgeries. Her intestine blockages required fourteen days of recovery. Imagine lying in a bed with numerous tubes in your body for drainage, infusions, and monitoring. Imagine that you cannot move and change your position to achieve a little comfort. Think about the severe thirst from all the medications and not being able to drink or swallow to satisfy that thirst. Imagine being unable to communicate about the pain from incisions.

For Joree's prior operations, Jillian and I traded every twelve hours throughout the recovery time. Since the nurses were not familiar with Joree's communication style, it was necessary to be with her to help them avoid her incessant moaning if she wasn't satisfied at the moment. They could not distinguish between pain and desire. After a week of this, we would both be exhausted. Sleeping in hospital recliners wears you out quickly, not to mention the institutional food. As the two-week mark approached, the "what's the point" thoughts grew larger in my thinking. I had become angry and anxious about the intrusion on our lives by the experience.

My thoughts were interrupted by a surgery nurse. "Mr. and Mrs. Harbeck, Dr. White asked me to come out and update you on the progress." She had our attention. "Joree is doing great. Dr. White is about halfway through the procedure, and it is going even better than expected. Her vital signs are strong. Dr. White anticipates it will be another hour before he is finished."

After we assured her we had no questions, she returned to the operating room. I remember the sense of relief. All the thoughts of futility and anger that I had just wrestled with fled in a second. Our Joree was doing well, and all signs were that the surgery was going to be successful.

It became very clear in that moment why Joree's life mattered. I felt horrible about my thoughts. How could I even consider believing her life was worthless? She came into this world without asking. Her disabilities were outside her control. Her original design was severely damaged through no fault of her own. But all the parts were there. There is a heart in her that beats just like everyone else's. She has a soul that was designed to relate with her creator. She belongs to God.

Not long after, Dr. White came into the waiting room looking very confident. "The surgery was a success," he said, smiling. "We were able to finish ahead of schedule. The rod is in place and doing its job. She will need to be sitting up in about an hour, after she recovers, to help with the fluids and the settling of the rod. Then it is just a matter of recovery time. We will follow up on her in a few weeks to be sure everything is working properly."

Jillian and I both shared the sense of relief. Now it was a matter of helping Joree through the painful recovery process. In addition to the rod that was wired to her spine, there were two large bolts drilled into her pelvis that held the rod in place. Dr. White used a new closing technique on the long incision. It was a type of organic superglue in lieu of traditional stitches. The glue held the wound in place and protected better against infection. It would dissolve in ten to fourteen days, leaving a thin scar and any further pain Joree would experience from it.

Jillian and I were waiting in the recovery room when the nurse wheeled Joree in. She was still sleeping. Her face was very puffy from the anesthesia. I counted ten different tubes that either provided her fluids and pain medication or drained other fluids and blood. It wasn't long before Joree moaned slightly. The nurse kept a close watch on her vital signs and the pain medication she was receiving. After about an hour, Joree was alert enough to be moved to her room in intensive care. Jillian was very tired, and I agreed to stay with Joree the first night. Once again, Joree showed what a courageous trooper she is.

The nurse spent about an hour arranging Joree's bed, along with all the monitors and tubes that would keep a watch on her through the night. Shortly thereafter, the nurses came in and informed me that the doctor ordered that they move Joree to a wheelchair, where she was to remain for sixty minutes. Not familiar with her normal conditions, the nurse asked if I would be willing to help get Joree into the chair. I cringed just thinking about it. How would we get under her back to lift her without injuring the incision? What about all the tubes and the transfer? I could tell the nurse was hesitant about the idea, so I offered to help.

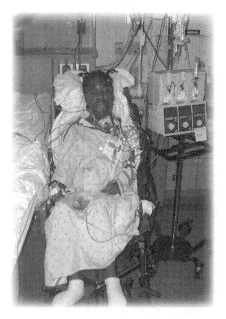

We carefully arranged all the tubes so none would get twisted or crimped on the transfer. I rolled Joree as gently as I could to see where I could place my arms for the lift. It took about ten minutes just to get everything in place to make the move. Joree's eyes were nearly swollen shut. I whispered in her ear that we were going to move her and I would be as careful as possible. In position, I counted to three and lifted her up, and then I transferred her to the chair. It only took a moment, but the whole time I felt awful having to move her. She moaned slightly as we placed her in the chair. We arranged the tubes and made her as comfortable as we could. The nurse smiled, and said she would be just outside if I needed her for anything. She reminded me that the doctor requested sixty minutes.

I sat as close to Joree as I could get, gently caressing her hand and her cheek. The time seemed to be moving ever so slowly; more than once, I wanted to just get her back in bed and comfortable. After forty-five minutes, she began to stir and tried to open her eyes. Then she moaned louder. I couldn't take it any longer. I buzzed the nurse and said I really wanted to get her back in bed and get her some more pain medication. The nurse agreed, and we worked again at organizing all the tubes. I could hear the pain and fatigue in Joree's moans. We tried to move quickly without rushing and injuring her more.

Finally, I got under her and lifted her back into bed. I placed several pillows around her side and back to cushion her as best I could. She was facing away from me. To my surprise, she turned her face toward me and whispered in a soft, gruff voice what I believe to this day were two words: "Thank you." I couldn't hold back the tears as Joree drifted off to sleep. What a champion. Just two hours after surgery, she had sat upright in a wheelchair for nearly an hour without a sound or moan. Every time I see the scar or think of that moment, I am reminded of her great courage.

Joree rested quietly that first night. The pain medication allowed her to sleep gently. I could have used some of that medicine myself. I sat next to her, marveling at all she had been through and what an example she was to me. Purpose? I had an answer for those who questioned her purpose. She is a child of the King. She was created in God's image. Sin, a part of this world, an enemy of God's creation, was responsible for her damaged body. Courage, determination, joy, and perseverance are also a part of his creation; Joree possesses those with equal measure. That day she once again demonstrated all of those traits to me and everyone who was a part of the surgery and recovery.

I considered for a while that had Jesus walked into her room that day, with his gentle and immeasurable compassion, he would have gently touched her broken body and made it well. One day, I mused, that will happen. For the time being, I knew he had his arms wrapped around her soul and was holding her tightly. I drifted off to sleep, feeling a sense of peace and safety in his love.

Unfortunately, Joree's journey is measured by the frequency and length of her hospital stays. After a three-year period of good health, Joree entered the hospital again on May 1, 2013, for her eleventh surgery.

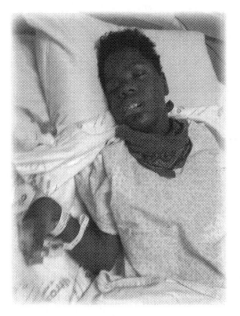

She spent twenty-eight days healing, twenty of those in the hospital. Staying in a hospital room for an extended period is a challenging experience. I have sat with Joree many times in hospital rooms, and I have been a surgery patient as well. Nurses and doctors come into your room every few hours to assess, poke, and stick. The nurse says, "If there is anything you need, you know where the call button is. Don't hesitate to ring me." So you ring them when the alarm button on the IV pump goes off at three o'clock in the morning, and they are nowhere to be found for twenty minutes. The first couple of days are spent recovering from surgery, a heart attack, or a broken bone, as the case may be, fading in and out of sleep and grateful for a morphine pump. By day five when the pain has eased, the routine quickly moves to monotony. You can only watch so much TV. If the stay extends beyond five days, claustrophobia becomes a condition, and if it goes beyond that, an erratic Jack Nicholson character starts coming to mind.

Later, Joree came home after a short (for her) ten-day stay at Paradise Valley Hospital. I'm not sure any of us would agree with the *Paradise* term, but the care was outstanding. It was so good to have her home again. So many of our friends had prayed for her surgery and recovery; we are extremely grateful.

As difficult as a hospital stay can be for anyone, imagine sitting ten days with a young lady who cannot speak. It is very difficult for both the patient and the caregivers. Someone must be with her twenty-four hours to assist the hospital staff with her care. Joree has a vocabulary of about fifteen words. *Ouch* is not one of them, so understanding her pain is something we have learned over the years. When Joree is in the hospital, we are in the hospital.

But as I reflected at the conclusion of the ten days, I realized once again that a hospital stay with Joree is like spending time with an angel. After three days she no longer required any pain medication, despite an eight-inch incision running vertically on her abdomen. Joree and I play a game with the word *no*. She says "no" and I respond with "no" in return. She changes the length of the word, adds a syllable, says it loudly or quietly, and I mimic her each time until she bursts into laughter. This causes me to respond with at least a grin, but usually with giggles or a burst of laughter. If you are near, it is almost impossible to be angry, upset, depressed, or anxious. Joree's presence and behavior just won't allow it.

In the hospital, this game goes on as long as Joree is awake and as long as you are in a confined space with her. At home, we come and go, and she cackles without engaging, but in the hospital there is no place to go. So ten days of saying "no" can lend itself to monotony. Not for Joree, however. I had never seen her so filled with joy. Nurses came in every six hours to stick her finger for blood. They took vital signs every four hours, waking Joree from a sound sleep. Some technicians repeatedly checked all the tubes in and out of her. Others executed breathing treatments, with a mask on her face and white vapor billowing around. And every moment, the smile, the laughter, the joy never waned.

I have thought long about how all this can be. How does she endure this so many times and never complain? Where does all that joy come from? She appears not to understand much of life as we know it, and yet her joy is constant. Our Lord was sent here to suffer. The whole reason for coming to Earth was to endure unimaginable pain and agony. The rest of the time, he demonstrated compassion, laughter, and joy, sharing it with a blind man, a lame man, a demon-possessed boy. I imagine that in those moments, the joy they experienced overwhelmed them. What was it like for Mary and Martha to see their brother walk out of that tomb?

Who is Joree, anyway? Don't you think it would be just like our Lord to see a child who is suffering from the curse of sin experience joy? Wouldn't it be just like him to send a helper to fill a broken body with joy? He did it himself. He came here to suffer and to endure death so we may have hope. Joree is a living, breathing example of our Lord. She didn't request a broken body. It isn't fair that she has to suffer while the rest of us go through life "normal." But what joy. We whine and moan about things every day that just don't go the way we desire. We worry, fret, and despair over things totally out of our control, and what do we get in return? Sadness, depression, anger, and frustration. So, who has this life thing figured out?

I believe more each day that Joree is an angel. Keep reading; I haven't gone over the edge. Do you have a better explanation? Our Lord knows suffering. Our Lord *loves*. Our Lord has no desire to see his image bearers suffer. Our Lord sees Joree, just as he sees you and me, and for some reason he has chosen her to be a shining example of joy, a joy that bolsters my faith. It challenges me when I go off on my own and believe I can manage this life thing by myself. Stay with Joree for a minute and she touches your heart. Walk with her for ten days in the hospital and it changes your soul. I can hear her right now as I write. She is babbling, she is laughing, she is singing. She is connected to our Lord, who is ever pursuing us and calling us home to be with him. I think that Joree, like an angel, is always there.

… Who told us we'd be rescued,
What has changed, and why should we be saved from nightmares?
We're asking why this happens to us who
have died to live, it's unfair …
This hand is bitterness, we want to taste and
let the hatred know, our sorrow …
Though eyes have opened slowly to lilies
of the valley and tomorrow …
This is what it means to be held,
how it feels when the sacred is torn from your life and you survive.
This is what it is to be loved and to know
that the promise was when everything fell, we'd be held.
—"Held," lyrics by Christa Nichole Wells

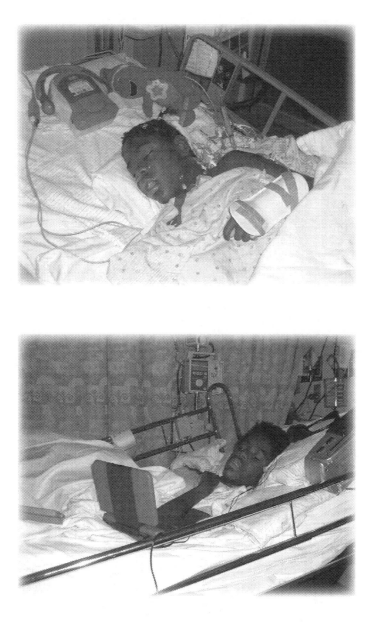

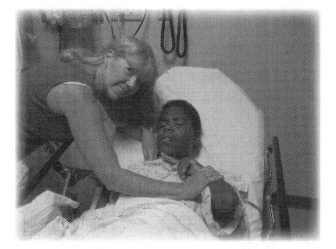

CHAPTER 6

Love Goes Both Ways

Over the years, on numerous occasions Jillian and I have heard this comment: "I don't know how you do this. I don't think I could ever do something like taking care of Joree. It is remarkable."

Frankly, as you have just read, this wasn't a planned endeavor. Joree came to us in the everyday course of life and we adapted with the flow. Our reaction to the comment is always to be a little uncomfortable. We didn't sit down and devise a plan to become foster parents. Joree came into our path and we made a decision to embrace her.

When any of us set out on this journey called life, we may have all the plans in the world, but at the start we have no idea how things will unfold. We get married and off we go. We have children. Each day we learn something new and challenging about them and us, and we adapt. That's why we often say, "If only I could have known then what I know now, I would have done things a lot differently."

When Joree arrived, we already had fourteen years of experience raising children. We never thought deeply about Joree's disabilities and what they would mean for her and us fifteen years down the road. She was here, and she needed a place to stay. And we had room. Jillian and I were blessed to be raised in Christian homes. We were taught from childhood that love for others is the core of Jesus' message. Jesus said, "I tell you the truth, whatever you did for one of the least of these brothers of mine, you did for me" (Matthew 25:40 ESV).

It is difficult to love well. So many factors enter into relationships that prevent us from loving each other unreservedly. Think of all the times someone has let you down. Someone abandoned you as a child or in a failing marriage. Maybe you were abused by a family member or someone very close to you, and trust issues prohibit you from loving well. Loving well requires that we remove any motives in our heart to love with even a hint of selfishness. We can't love well if we say, "I will love you, but I sure better see something in return," or "I'm not putting myself out on the line for you if I am never going to get anything back."

Jillian and I and the children have learned over the years that Joree really loves well. You might ask, How can that be? She has a vocabulary of a few words and can't formulate a sentence. She can't reach out and hug or kiss you. If she can't speak or touch, how in the world does she love well?

One way to measure how well someone loves is to look at how the person receives the love you show to him or her. Joree has taught us that we can love her without her ever having to do anything to deserve it, and when we do, she accepts it without condition.

A good way to show love to people is to accept their love—period. We get tangled up in the idea that we can or must do something for people in order for them to love us. Jesus was so clear that this is untrue. He called us children, little children at that, and he explained to us that there is nothing we can do to earn his love. We must just receive it. In return for the uninvited love, I can choose to say thank you. You see, it is always about the heart. Pure love loves without any expectation of something in return. We love Joree, knowing very well there is nothing she can do for us in return. Joree loves us by receiving it. Love goes both ways.

When I am loved without condition, I am left with nothing more than gratitude and saying thank you. Your response of *thank you* is a gift of love in return that I must receive as well. In turn, I must say, "No, thank *you* for thanking me." And then you respond by saying, "No, thank you for thanking me for thanking you." And on and on it goes. We can experience the same dynamic with God. We thank him for our life, health, and well-being. He in return thanks us for our obedience. When we practice that give and take with God, it is called praise, and it only comes from a pure heart.

As Jerry B. Jenkins says, "Love is not a state of being. It's an act of the will. It cannot be demanded or required or commanded. It can only be bestowed" (*Twelve Things I Want My Kids to Remember* [Moody Press, 1991], 24).

When Joree came into our family's life many years ago, Jillian and I did not think at the time about the future—hers or ours. We met a little girl in need of care and we welcomed her into our family. This book is a celebration of her life. It is a tribute to all parents and caregivers that daily give of themselves and walk through life with the special ones among us.

Joree's disabilities are severe. If she could speak to you, I am quite sure she would minimize her condition. She would challenge you to consider living with joy. Joree and millions of disabled people have little, if anything, to show to the world. They have no degrees, no reputation, no influence, no connections with influential people; they do not create much, produce much, or earn much. They tend to be hidden away from public view. Yet despite her extreme limitations, Joree awakens every single day smiling. In fact, she smiles all day long.

How can that be? How does a person who can't speak, walk, eat, or do anything else for herself spend the entire day being happy? I can guess, but I can't be certain of the reasons for her infectious personality. What I do know is that her joy has challenged Jillian and I since the moment we met her.

All these years she has demonstrated complete dependence. Every moment of her life, she is dependent on us and her caregivers to manage every experience and activity of life. Without it, she would perish. Without ever saying a word, she demonstrates what it means to surrender, to submit, to leave all you have with someone else and trust them to care.

The label utilized to identify the disabled has evolved over the years in an attempt to soften the perception of the brokenness. It has changed from retarded, to handicapped, to disabled, and now to special. I don't believe we need to change it ever again.

Joree truly is a special person. She has been teaching our family from the day we met what it means to love. Love is resting in the arms of the one who will care for you with no reservations and no conditions.

Joree has been with Jillian, me, and the rest of our family for twenty-three years now. I have related just a tiny bit of the years of experiences we have shared. We have learned from Joree what it means to love well. In the second part of the book, we want to share the other lesson Joree has taught us: what it means to be dependent.

PART II

Embracing Dependence

CHAPTER 7

Joree and Jillian

You never know when the circumstances of life will change you forever. After thirteen years of marriage, my wife, Jillian, began to suffer with a debilitating health issue that rendered her nearly bedridden for two years. In the rest of this chapter, Jillian writes of her experiences before and after she encountered Joree.

The year was 1987. Life was grand. I was happily married to a wonderful man and had three wonderful children. Like everyone, we were wrapped up in the crazy, busy, rat-race schedule. Life was good-except for some persistent, painful, and annoying female problems. The symptoms lingered nearly a year. My doctor told me that in order to have the pain and general fatigue go away, a hysterectomy was necessary. *Hmmm,* I thought. *Okay, let's get this surgery over with so my happy, busy life can resume on schedule.* Being a nurse with a positive attitude, I knew I could have the surgery, bounce back, and probably have even more energy than ever.

Bill and I talked with the kids and assured them everything would be fine. I was admitted to Central DuPage Hospital in June 1988 for an abdominal hysterectomy. The surgery went well, and everything seemed to be going fine until about ten o'clock that night, when I hemorrhaged. I was rushed into emergency surgery, and the outcome left me very, very sick. I remember thinking, *I'd rather be dead than have to deal with this pain.* Seven days later, following two blood transfusions and numerous pain medications, I was released from the hospital. I was very weak and not sure if I would ever feel normal again.

The recovery was slow and exhausting, and I wrestled with God about my condition: *God, you have to give me back my strength. I have so much to do.* I was working; I was a mom, a wife, an exercise instructor; my kids were in activities that required me. I had singing engagements; my house needed attention; I was a room mother; and on and on. God had another plan for me, and I was not even close to understanding or accepting it.

You would think that since I was a nurse I would know better, but I thought, *Aah, just two weeks more; I will take it easy and I will be just like new.* That was my plan, or so I thought. Instead, the summer of 1988 turned out to be the worst summer of my life. I relinquished some control and acknowledged that maybe God was trying to get my attention.

There I was, with zero energy. The more I tried, the more tired I became. My stubborn streak convinced me that in just five weeks I could return to work. I told myself that I could keep up no matter what. Instead, over the next year, I suffered a physical, emotional, and spiritual breakdown.

Eventually, I was confined to bed eighteen to twenty hours a day, a condition that would last almost two years. Now, all you wives and moms, think of what life would be like for your family in that situation. After months and months of tests and doctor visits, I was finally diagnosed with chronic fatigue syndrome. I also had fibromyalgia (which is like arthritis, only it attacks the muscles). Unfortunately, there was no remedy at the time. My doctor's orders were to slow down my lifestyle, rest, and take medication.

Slowly, I developed depression, mostly caused by the constant flu-like symptoms and inability to function. I maintained a low-grade fever; every muscle in my body ached. I couldn't concentrate; I didn't care about anything or anyone; and all I wanted to do (and did) was cry. I felt guilty for not being able to function as a wife and mom. Additionally, it was during this time that the patient I had been caring for died. She was only thirty-eight years old. I was thirty-six years old, and I remember one night telling Bill, very seriously, that it would be better for him and the kids if I would just die too. Wow, that scared Bill a lot. It was December 1990.

Shortly thereafter, Bill took me to a counselor. I thought I was going to see another medical doctor. That day I started antidepressant medication. You see, depression hit me like a brick because of the physical limitations that the condition developed. Satan almost got a strong hold on me but instead, God had obtained my attention. God doesn't do random. This was a heart check. Did I truly believe in God's Word and trust him? If so, it was time to listen and try to understand what he expected from me. God literally stopped me completely so I would listen. I was always so busy and "full speed ahead" that I didn't take any time out to really listen to God. The third letter of John, verse 2, says, "Dear Friend, I am praying that all is well with you and that your body is as healthy as I know your soul is" (TLB).

After years of doctors, and numerous treatment regiments, I slowly recovered to manageable levels. I share this because I am convinced that if I had not gone through all my physical setbacks, I would never have accepted Joree being a part of my life and family. Joree was born in January 1991, near the time I began healing. We met her six months later. God's timing is the best. His plan was to allow Joree to be a part of our family, and as of April 22, 1996, she legally became our daughter.

I reflect often on the many wonderful memories we have about Joree. Her addition to our family has proven God's love and faithfulness. God has used Joree as part of my own healing and allowed me enough strength to love her and care for all her physical needs. The best part is being blessed by her daily smile and the joy she adds to experiences—family, church, holidays, birthdays, vacations, school, and so many others. We observed her take small steps of progress, and we rejoiced. She learned to hum to her favorite music. She learned to use her favorite toy using just one finger. To communicate simple needs, she began to use words and short phrases such as *music, toy, video,* and *ice.* Though it is not clear to many, she has learned to count to ten. Her favorite saying when at the mall is "I want to go home."

Communication is the hardest for all of us, but we have learned her needs by her looks and sounds. Joree has been working now for awhile using a communication device that assists her in speaking by the push of a button. Her facial responses show clearly her satisfaction that we understand each other.

I have learned a few things about myself. I am realizing I tend to put a lot of pressure on myself to never say no to anyone or anything. God gives us opportunities, but sometimes I go full speed ahead and again forget to stop and listen to God's plan for a particular opportunity.

I felt I could go back to work full-time. From the moment Joree had joined our family, I had been aware of her total dependency on me to care for her. This kept me from overbooking my life. Her constant physical needs forced me to observe life from the perspective of just how good we were for each other. With Joree in school, however, I again had open time during the school day. My restlessness motivated me to find something to keep me busy and help others. That's what nurses do. I once again found myself overcommitting at work until I was unable to function at all. I had slipped back into overdoing it and trying to live in my own strength.

By 2005 I was once again feeling physical effects. I consulted with my doctor, and after blood work was done, it was confirmed that I had chronic lymphocytic leukemia, a type of cancer. The word cancer gets your attention quickly. I have left the workplace completely. Just as Joree taught Bill about dependence, she is teaching me. I must lean on Bill and my family when my desire is to keep moving and serving but I must stop. It's about releasing control into the arms of others.

We are told that God knows what is best for our life. I am sure everyone can look back on an event or situation that at the time was devastating. Years later though, we see it as God's plan—his best plan for our life. The first letter to the Corinthians says, "I know when I see Jesus face to face; I will understand totally every reason He allowed this in my life" (1 Corinthians 13:12, my paraphrase). Right now, looking back, I know it was his only way to stop me and teach me to listen, learn, and depend on him. God allowed this for me. I could not always say that. Now, I say it and mean it from my heart: *Thank you, Lord, for allowing the trials in my life to grow and strengthen my love and trust in you.*

My soul is healthier today, and my body is functioning, with some limitations. Sleep, medication, and warm weather help me feel comfortable. I still need reminders from my family about when to slow down, rest, and go average-speed ahead. But I am so thankful for the daily strength God allows me to have, because I know it is not mine alone.

CHAPTER 8

A Wounded Soul

On April 22, 1996, five years after Joree had first joined us, Jillian, Jeff, Julee, and I stood before a judge of the Circuit Court of Cook County in Chicago, Illinois, and heard him pronounce that from that day forward, Joree's name would be Joree Jeanine Harbeck. She would have all the rights and privileges of our other three children. She was officially our daughter. Those five years taught us as a family that love is not something you fall into—it is something you do. Joree had affected all of us, and it was time to make official what we all already knew. She was our family. What I didn't know at the time was the impact, just two months later, that this little girl was going to have on my life forever.

I was working as a high school principal in Aurora, Illinois. We had moved to Aurora the previous year to be closer to the school. This was about two years before our move to Phoenix that I described in the first part of the book. Joree was five years old and attending a local preschool for children with special needs. She was adapting well to the three-day-a-week program as they attempted to work with her physical challenges as well as communication skills. At this time, she did not speak any words. Life had settled into a comfortable routine. But things were about to explode.

It was a Friday afternoon, and Jillian and I had arranged to have a meal together at an Olive Garden restaurant in Aurora. Jaimee, now eighteen years old, and Jeff, sixteen, agreed to stay home with Julee and Joree so Jillian and I could go out together. I had been battling the last few years with darkness and depression in my soul that had reached a breaking point. Sitting in the restaurant, just after we ordered our food, I blurted out to Jillian that I had been sexually abused as a child.

She appeared astonished and confused. She paused and looked at me. "What did you say?"

I could barely get the words out again through the emotion. "I was sexually abused as a child." For years, the toxic shame had been tearing away at my soul more intensely than ever before. I had reached a point where something had to be done. I had wrestled with going on. In fact, on many days, I had contemplated going away, running away—even ending it all to escape the pain in my soul.

I broke into sobs as a flood of emotion came pouring out. It grew to the point that we had to leave the restaurant. In the car, the flood of tears continued for a long time as Jillian sat with me. When I was finally able to speak, I shared with her just a few details of my past dark secret. We had been married nearly twenty-three years and it was the first time she had ever heard this. She was the first person in my life who ever heard the secret. The sense of relief that came in that moment is indescribable. Finally, the darkness that I had carried for so long was out. All the years of protective behaviors were in the open. All the years of trying to control my world to keep it safe were out of my hands. The deepest, darkest pain and the bondage to that pain were lifted for a moment, and it felt incredible. It was finally out. I was free. Now I could live.

Jillian recalls that day and what she subsequently learned about my past. Here is her account:

> One day in May, Bill met me for lunch when he was principal of Aurora Christian School. I did not realize it at the time, but our world was about to be flipped upside down with the heartfelt words Bill tearfully shared with me. It is hard to explain, but I felt God's peace and comfort along with almost unspeakable shock, as I listened to him speak so emotionally. Bill shared with me how at age twelve, a trusted family member on visits to his parents' home sexually abused him. I remember thinking at the time, *How in the world was this innocent young boy able to take all this new and confusing emotion and be able to discern what was happening to him?*
>
> The abuse persisted. The abuser told Bill never to speak of this "special connection" to anyone, especially his parents. As I listened, my heart and soul were screaming out with intense anger. Yet I wanted to hug and comfort

Bill at the same time. Here we were at what I had thought would be a normal dinner out at a restaurant, and I was hearing how thirty years earlier, my husband of twenty-three years was abused over and over and over again. We both felt the heavy emotion of it all, and the tears kept flowing.

Over the next few days and weeks, my questions increased. I slowly began to understand the reasons for Bill's moodiness, hours of silence, and ever-changing personality traits. I continued to realize, little by little, just how much damage this horrible abuse had brought to my husband's entire life. I saw how it affected every person he came in contact with, every choice that was given to him, every decision he had to make, and every emotion that faced him. His entire personality and his ability to interact with others were deeply wounded. Our journey to healing after the first conversation moved very, very slowly.

As Bill's wife, what was I going to do to help him? How and where should we begin this difficult walk? My mind went in circles and my heart raced. I could hardly breathe. Thoughts and verses came to me as if God came down and spoke them directly in my ear: *Marriage is not about perfection. It is about unity—blending strengths and forgiving weaknesses to become together what neither could alone.* I recalled 1 Peter 3:1–7 regarding how husbands and wives should treat each other.

I was concerned for many years that my behavior as a secretive abuse survivor had affected my children in ways that would surface in their own lives later. I was worried that I had unintentionally impacted their lives in a negative way because of my coping behaviors. I felt guilty about having been so selfishly entrenched in my status as a victim that I failed them as a father. I had made it a point to be physically present in their lives, never missing events, always spending time, making family moments. But when they told me they always felt something was wrong, I feared my wrong behaviors would surface in their lives.

Jillian felt it was critical for us to share the story with the children. It was difficult for them to understand or relate to the pain I had endured. Yet each of them had sensed as they grew up that there was something about Dad that was mysterious. They weren't sure what it was, but they sensed it. Upon hearing the story, their hearts reached out in a new way to me that was genuine, loving, and supportive. We can't go back and fix those days for them. Their unconditional love has been a blessing and healing potion for both Jillian and me.

It wasn't until I included Jillian in the journey that I was able to begin healing. I now tell any survivor of abuse, "You have to tell your story. Don't keep it inside; share it with someone you love and the world. It isn't easy, but it is truly the way to hope."

The children and I have had the opportunity to talk about those days. They have demonstrated understanding and compassion toward me that has humbled me in ways they will never know. All three were curious why I never told them. Why I allowed it to happen without getting help. They wished I had opened up to them sooner. I told them the great fear of losing their respect and their love kept me from telling them. What became clear was that they were now modeling for me what redemption means. They were angry about what happened;

they were disappointed I didn't trust them to confide in them; but they extended unconditional love and grace to me and have become a major part of my journey of healing.

A number of years later, in 2006, when we were in Phoenix, Arizona, I was serving as an assistant to the superintendent in a large Christian school. He was planning to retire, and I was nearing the day when I would replace him as superintendent. In March of that year, I was approached by a ministry that provided awareness and healing for survivors of sexual abuse. After prayer and discussion, Jillian and I decided I would accept a position as an employee of the ministry. I was eight years into my healing journey. I believed this was a God-ordained opportunity to advance the word about the damage of sexual abuse and to open doors for healing.

One year into the ministry work, however, I was diagnosed with prostate cancer. During the nine-week treatment period, the leaders of the ministry communicated to me that my position was no longer needed. I was devastated. But it was out of my control.

I spent four months resting and recuperating from the cancer treatment. In March 2008, Jillian and I launched a new nonprofit ministry to continue the work I had become passionate about. I was quite confident that everyone would embrace the message and support the cause.

Eight months into the new work with our ministry, I suffered a massive heart attack. *Are you kidding?* I thought. Again, I had no control over any of the circumstances. I was dependent—on God's grace.

What has become very clear is the example Joree has been for me in my healing. She is completely dependent. If we didn't feed her, she would starve in a short time. If we didn't change her diaper or change her position in bed on a regular basis, she would suffer from disease or skin breakdown. She waits on every move. She is the truth of surrendering to dependence.

I have learned (usually the hard way) how much Joree influences me to let go of the control I so desire. Letting go means vulnerability. Letting go requires dependence on those outside you to care about you without conditions. Letting go requires one to place his or her life in others' hands. For an abuse survivor who has experienced a broken trust in the most personal area of life, to let go is nearly impossible. Joree rested in our hands from the day she arrived, and every day she reminds me I must surrender to the truth of dependence.

The healing road has been a journey of pain and more pain. It has been about rebuilding trust. Joree and I have traveled this path together, her in her physical struggles and I in my soul pain. She is an image of Christ in her suffering and joy. She has taught me what it means to be dependent. She continues to teach me what it means to hope.

In 2008, I published a book called *Shattered: One Man's Journey from Sexual Abuse*. It is my story of abuse and healing. This supports the mission of the nonprofit organization. Jillian and I also operate a home we call the Hope House. It is a safe place for fellow survivors to come, tell their story, mourn the many things they have lost, and begin the healing journey. For those who come to heal, they have the opportunity to meet and interact with Joree. Without ever saying a word, Joree opens hearts to the truth of dependence.

CHAPTER 9

There Is Joy in Surrender

We humans do not ponder much the concept of dependence. Why? Because from the moment we are born, we seek independence. I observed all of my children, and now all of my grandchildren, making the following statements repeatedly: "I can do this myself." "Leave me alone." "Get out of my way." The crazy thing is they all started it at the ripe old age of two. A conflict rages in us every moment of life between the need to believe we are in control and the desperate fear of feeling lost, between a determination to influence the world around us on our terms and the perpetual need to believe we are loved.

According to the Bible, this constant clash originated between Adam and Eve in the garden of Eden. Imagine a CNN reporter offering an interview to this very first couple for the nightly news. The journalist's first question is, "So, Mr. Adam, you have been living here with your wife now for some time. Tell me, what do you depend on?"

You can picture Adam with a quizzical look on his face, searching for a way to respond. Finally, he says, "Well, we don't depend on anything. Everything we could ever want or need, we have. I'm not sure where you even came up with that question. We have everything."

Designed into the first couple was the heart of their creator. God designed them to be a mirror image of his glory: "God the Father, Son, and Spirit want for nothing, and you, as our creation—you will want for nothing. You will live in total freedom. You will experience our glory in the physical realm of intimacy. You will forever be in paradise. When you have children together, you will teach others the picture of a family. You will have power over all the earth and you will multiply. This is all yours."

Then the unthinkable happened. In an instant everything changed. Adam and Eve had it all, when along came a new idea that they had not heard. It wasn't a new design or plan. They were presented with just a simple question: "Do you think God is hiding something from you? He said you would die if you don't obey him. Come on, he wouldn't do that to you. He has given you everything; he wouldn't hold something back."

I'm not sure how long it was that Eve pondered that question. Did she mull it over repeatedly, wondering if her creator had held something back? Was the allure to do something on her own, apart from God, too compelling to continue being faithful? Did she discuss it with Adam before she made her decision? All we know is that she had a moment of doubt, and she forsook her dependence to strike out on her own. And her husband joined her. From that moment to this time, we doubt.

There are many days when I dream and hope that I could experience paradise even for just a moment. Instead, worry, disappointment, and discouragement occupy my days and nights while the never-ending frustration of making a living and demonstrating the appearance that I have it all together often drives me to exhaustion. Day after day, I work. It feels as if I am filling up giant water jugs, only to discover in the morning that they have tiny holes in them and the water leaks out. Still, I return the next day to do it again, and again.

Inside each of us is the daily struggle of believing that we are and must be in control of all of life around us—around "me." Adam and Eve's sin passed the curse on to every human. With the curse comes the little thread of doubt. We just aren't quite sure if God, parents, teachers, and all others are holding out on us. For protection, we do whatever we must to be safe. I just can't trust anyone. At the same time, there is a deep, deep desire to love and be loved. But if I don't trust you, how can I love you and you love me?

Is there a way to control the madness? This will not be over for any of us until we die. We cannot remove the curse in this life that haunts us every waking moment. We will strive every day to fight the burning desire to be in control—some days, we will win, and some days, we will lose. We will long every day to love well, but we will do this only inconsistently. We will doubt that God is really on our side or that God is there for us when things go bad. We will battle shame and guilt, convinced we can never measure up to a standard we think God requires. We will run ourselves ragged doing good things that help the world and feel really good about it—only to wake up the next morning wondering if it was worth the effort. We are a mess. We are broken people. We must surrender to being dependent.

Joree is twenty-three years old now. She has been dependent since the day she was born. She has no understanding of her dependence. Like Adam and Eve when they were placed in the garden, all she knows is that everything she needs is taken care of for her every minute of every day. She is a picture of the intent of the original design. God requested from us that we rest in him. We wanted to go it alone. We suffer every time we attempt to do life ourselves. We will not understand how to let go completely until our lives are over. On that day, Joree's arms and legs will work again. Her tongue will speak. She will be free. On that day, we will cease the battle and we will allow our creator to be our all.

What can we do until that day comes? Surrender to the truth of dependence. For Jillian and I believe Joree would tell you two things. First, every waking moment, be grateful, and second, be kind. It is impossible to be selfish and independent when you are giving to others with a heart of love and saying thank you for every breath you breathe.

It has taken a few years to write this account, because her story with us continues. Joree is our sweet and joyful daughter. She is our inspiration to continue to feel the best kind of love and compassion for others on a daily basis. We hope she will inspire you to love well.

I'm limited … just look at me … I'm limited …
and just look at you, you can do all I couldn't do,

I've heard it said, that people come into our lives for a reason,
Bringing something we must learn
And we are led to those who help us most to grow,

If we let them, and we help them in return
Well I don't know if I believe that's true
But I know I'm who I am today because I knew you

Like a comet pulled from orbit as it passes a sun
Like a stream that meets a bolder, halfway through the wood
Who can say if I've been changed for the better
But because I knew you ...
I have been changed for good ...

—"For Good," lyrics by Stephen Schwartz

APPENDIX 1

Special Tributes from Family

Our children have each been affected in different ways. Living with a person with disabilities awakens your mind and heart to the fragile nature of life. It has given our children an appreciation for their freedom and health. They possess sensitivity toward others that Jillian and I could not teach them with just words. They have experienced compassion, and it has molded their souls for the rest of their lives. While not all of them have chosen to continue actively caring for children in foster care or with special needs, Julee chose a career path in special education. Certainly, growing up with Joree, her sister, had a little influence on that decision. Jaimee, Jeff, and Julee, now as adults, demonstrate daily the understanding and heart of compassion they learned by welcoming Joree into their family. Aah, the grace of God.

In this book, you've heard my perspective primarily. Here, we include thoughts from Joree's siblings as well as her nieces and nephews. Jillian also provides some reflections.

Jaimee Draper—One of Joree's Older Sisters

Over the year years, the thing I have observed most about my parents caring for Joree is sacrifice. There have been multiple blessings, lessons, and joy, but with all of them have come tremendous sacrifice.

I remember being apprehensive about having Joree in our home. She required so much care that I thought it would only take away from my time with my parents. I felt at times that there was no way they'd be able to be there for me if they were exhaustively caring for Joree's needs. What I found, though, was that the Lord had some things to teach me through it all.

God taught me to share my time and not make it all about me. He showed me that we are called to care for those in need. He

showed me that we literally are to take care of those who Jesus called "the least of these." I learned, by watching my parents, how to let go of my agenda for the day and let the Lord lead us where he plans. I learned, by watching my parents, that sleepless nights again and again are worth it, despite the accompanying pain and weariness. Sacrifice. I learned that it is all worth it, because it is not in vain.

All of it—the emptying of self, the giving, the serving of others in need—is unto the Lord, for his sake. That lesson is an eternal one, because when we meet the Lord, that will be something that matters. We will meet Jesus face to face and answer to him. He paid the ultimate sacrifice on the cross. That sacrifice is hard to comprehend, but the picture of giving of one's self to care for someone in need is a small picture of what Jesus did by caring for me. He forgave my sin when I couldn't care for it myself. He sacrificially took the pain I deserved, and beyond sleepless nights and weariness, he died for me. I am grateful for what I have seen and learned through Joree and my parents. God will have his way in us, and I am thankful to be able to call Joree my sister.

Jeff Harbeck—Joree's Older Brother

I remember, from the moment my parents first brought this special baby home, that there was never any reservation in my heart about her being a part of our family. I felt protective of her almost immediately. When my parents sat us down to ask us our feelings on Joree becoming a permanent member of our family, it was without hesitation that I wanted to be her big brother. She had so much joy, despite her limitations. Her smiling face was lifting the spirits of everyone in the family, most notably my mom, who had been battling a fatigue illness for quite some time. Joree felt like a natural fit in our family from the very beginning. It was easy to be drawn to this joyful personality. I remember wanting to sit with her, make her laugh, and soak up some of her happiness that seemed almost contagious. This sometimes meant watching her favorite movies repeatedly, such as *The Little Mermaid* and *Beauty and the Beast*, the dialogue of which I can still recite word for word and impress my own children today. She's always been soothed by music and sing-a-longs, which was another reason why she belonged in our musical family.

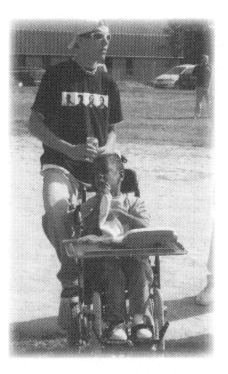

One of my most cherished childhood memories was the day our family stood in the Circuit Court of Cook County and Joree's last name became Harbeck. It was official, and nobody could take her away from us.

My outlook on people with special needs was affected greatly by having Joree as my sister. I learned about interacting with children or adults with disabilities. I learned to have compassion for them and even volunteered at special-needs school during my high school years, simply because I thought it was fun to hang out with them. I cannot imagine life without my sister Joree. She has shaped each member of my family in a unique way. I am truly grateful to God that she was brought into my family's life.

Julee Hoffner—Joree's Other Older Sister

It is impossible to cram into just a few paragraphs a lifetime of memories of my sister Joree. Instead, with my greatest effort, I will try to express the incredible impact she has had on my life as a sister, a friend, an inspiration, and a blessing.

I do not remember my life without Joree. I was seven years old when she came into our family. What I remember most in the first few years of knowing Joree was that she was the happiest person I knew. I loved to make her laugh, and in return she would do the same for me. I instantly embraced the role of big sister. You see, I was the youngest sibling and always "the little sister." When Joree arrived, I finally got to be the big sister. It was new and exciting. I felt proud to hold this new responsibility. Being a sister would never be the same. I loved helping Joree whenever she needed it, whether it was feeding her, clothing her, bathing her, or just sitting on the couch snuggling, watching a video. She was my little sister, and nothing would ever change that.

As time went on, and Joree and I both grew older, we began to develop a different kind of relationship. Joree trusted me as her caregiver, playmate, and entertainer; but the trust grew into a friendship. We began to develop a bond that would last a lifetime. Trust is imperative in a relationship with an individual with disabilities. Over time, I began to understand Joree better and how her disability implied a sense of vulnerability. There were only a certain few people who Joree felt safe with, and I was one of them. This friendship, including an understanding of who Joree was and all that she was capable of, jumpstarted a process that would eventually lead to my career.

I know that the Lord placed Joree in my parents' hands for a number of reasons. I had no idea that one reason was to open a door to a whole new perspective on what I wanted to do professionally. I am a special education teacher. I work with individuals like Joree every day, and I believe it is the most rewarding job. Without Joree, I could have easily overlooked people with disabilities, or worse, not respected them and their ability. I have had countless students come and go, leaving a lasting impact. I learn more from them than they could ever learn from me. I know Joree played a key role in this process.

The Lord challenges me daily in many ways. I am thankful for those challenges, because they strengthen my relationship and dependence on my Lord and Savior Jesus Christ. Joree is a constant reminder of struggle and dependence. While she relies completely on others for support and care, she does it without complaint, and always with a smile.

I believe Joree is a good example of how Christ wants us to live. We will struggle, we need to depend on the Lord, and we need to give him all of the glory, because at the end of the day that is all that matters. Romans 5:3–5 says, "More than that, we rejoice in our sufferings, knowing that suffering produces endurance, and endurance produces character, and character produces hope, and hope does not put us to shame, because God's love has been poured into our hearts through the Holy Spirit who has been given to us."

Joree has been such a blessing in my life. I am thankful that she is my sister, my friend, and a continuing inspiration in my life.

Joree's Nieces and Nephews—Jakob, Jaylin, Payson, Lola, London, Noah, and Oakley

Bill and I are blessed with seven grandchildren, who each have a special connection to their Auntie Joree. I spent time talking with the children about their relationships with Auntie Joree. This section reflects what they shared with me.

In spite of all her limitations, Joree enjoys life. She loves to go to sporting events. She screeches with delight, cheering along with the crowd. She enjoys being with children of all ages. I believe she feels a part of the action, and when children approach her, she always greets them with her infectious smile.

From the earliest days, music has been an important part of her daily life. When Joree was a baby, we would play all of the children's favorite Sunday school songs. As Joree grew older, we would hear her humming with her favorite tunes, and she was on key! Not long after, she learned to express herself in a special way, informing us that certain songs were her favorite. She insisted they be placed on the repeat button for long periods. Naturally, we couldn't help but hum or sing along with her. The delightful music would actually change our moods into joy. Even to the present time, the songs continue to bring smiles to us even on bad days. Love goes both ways.

Along with music, videos are a constant form of entertainment. When Joree was two years old, we learned that all the *Barney and Friends* videos were her favorite. She was attracted once again to the upbeat music in the videos. As she grew older, we were all delighted when she added *Dora the Explorer* to her watch list and discovered Disney: *Beauty and the Beast, The Little Mermaid, 101 Dalmatians, Dumbo,* and others.

Time has allowed us the joy of grandchildren. Auntie Joree is a valuable person in each of their developing lives. We have enjoyed watching each of the grandkids interact with their aunt and learn about her disabilities. From the time they could sit with her in her bed and watch videos with her, they have demonstrated curiosity, compassion, and lack of fear. Every one of the seven have learned from the start that Auntie Joree is different, but each has approached her without trepidation and with an understanding of her limitations that will transfer into their everyday lives.

I remember clearly when Jaylin (Jaimee and Jason's daughter) was about eighteen months old; she was watching *The Little*

Mermaid while the rest of the family was visiting in the family room. All of a sudden, I felt a tug on my shorts. Eventually I looked down and noticed that Jaylin definitely wanted my attention. I picked her up and gave her a big hug and kiss, but that wasn't what she wanted. She looked very serious as she pointed to Joree's room. Obviously, she wanted me to accompany her there immediately. As we walked through the door, it was apparent that Joree was moaning and needed something. As Jaylin and I approached her, I asked Joree, "What would you like, my sweet little girl?"

Jaylin had already tried to give Joree a certain musical toy, but it appeared Jaylin couldn't reach the toy and felt Joree really wanted it. I looked at Joree and then at Jaylin. I asked her, "Is that the toy you think Joree wants but you can't quite reach it?"

Jaylin smiled and clapped as I picked up the toy. Jaylin wanted to bring the joy to Joree herself. She walked over to Joree's bed, climbed on a chair, reached over, and gave her the toy. To my amazement, Joree gave Jaylin a huge smile. I am sure Joree was thinking, "Thank you so much, Jaylin. Nana didn't hear me, but you did a great job of getting her for me." With both girls happy, Jaylin crawled up next to Joree on her bed and placed a stuffed animal by her head. They enjoyed the rest of *The Little Mermaid* together.

There are so many stories. I was caring for our oldest grandson, Jakob, while his mother was working. Jakob, age three, told me he thought Joree would like to watch a video. "What video would you and Auntie Joree like to watch together?" I asked him. He looked at me with absolute certainty as he handed me a *Bob the Builder* tape. "Well, let's ask Joree what she thinks, Jake," I said. I placed the *Bob the Builder* cover in front of Joree and said, "Would you like to watch *Bob the Builder* with Jakob first and then maybe a *Barney* video for the next one?"

Joree heard the word *Barney* and gave a big smile. I got Jakob set up in a chair with a little table next to Joree's bed, handed him a snack, and started the video. After giving Joree one of her favorite toys, I started to leave the room, when Jakob stopped me. He said, "Nana, where is Joree's treat?" I could see he was a bit troubled that he not only got to choose the video but received a treat as well. I was touched by his caring about Joree's situation as well. After I explained that I would give her something later, he seemed satisfied and watched the video happily for the next thirty minutes. Joree was just content to have her little nephew sitting in her room with her. As I walked away, she smiled with delight.

As each of the grandchildren grew, they surpassed Joree's mental and physical abilities. I witnessed how growing up together with Joree had such a positive influence on all of them.

Our oldest daughter, Jaimee, and her husband, Jason, moved to Arizona the same time we did in 1998. While here, they were blessed with our first grandson, Jakob, and our first granddaughter, Jaylin. In 2009 they moved back to Illinois to take a position in a new church. It was hard to see them leave, but the attachment the children made with their Aunt Joree has left them always asking about her and having wonderful memories of their time with her. When I talk about Jake and Jaylin to Joree, she shows a little sparkle in her eyes, expressing to me she remembers and misses them as well. When they come for a visit, I know Joree remembers them.

Most recently, our youngest daughter, Julee, and her husband, Ryan, had their first child, born in Arizona in 2012. We are delighted to have Noah close by to spoil. Every time he comes over, his first look is to see if Joree is home. He heads straight for her room. If she is not there, he looks inquisitively at me as if to say, "Where is Auntie Joree?" When I tell Noah that Joree has gone to her day program, he isn't satisfied until I pick him up and we go to her picture on the wall. It is only then that you hear a little giggle of joy as he smiles at her picture.

If Joree is home, Noah loves to sit on her bed with her to watch movies, listen to music, or play with her toys. I believe he intuitively understands that something is not quite right, but he is learning from the start that Auntie Joree is very special.

Our son, Jeff, and his wife, Alanna, live in Illinois. Their three kids, Payson, Lola, and London, have shared limited time with Auntie Joree. As with their cousins, when they visit, they demonstrate the innocence of children as well as their unconditional love and understanding. They are captivated by Joree's joyful countenance. The time with her will shape and mold their understanding of the world and of love.

I don't really know how much Joree understands. I do see that when the grandchildren are near, she demonstrates more joy than usual. I know that the grandchildren are influenced for good. I know that in a world of brokenness, for a moment the kids and Joree share the journey. Love goes both ways.

APPENDIX 2

In Recognition of Caregivers

Traveling the day-to-day road with Joree wears you down at times. Imagine an infant in your care 365 days a year for more than two decades. It is physically and emotionally challenging. Often it is tiresome. We have a lifelong appreciation for parents and caregivers of children and adults with disabilities. Given the twenty-four-hour care Joree needs, it is wonderful that over the years we have had the blessing of kind and compassionate caregivers to allow us a break at times.

Joree began attending school at age seven, and in each of the schools, she has had teachers that were committed to children with special needs. Six to eight hours a day during the school year, Joree interacted with teachers, students with disabilities, and regular education students. Joree now attends a wonderful day program for adults with disabilities. She continues to progress slowly and loves going every day.

Joree can never be left alone. Therefore, when she is not in school or a day program, someone must be with her. That can be very limiting indeed. We moved to Arizona in 1998, and for the last eleven years, we have had marvelous caregivers. Two women have gone above and beyond in caring for Joree. This has allowed us opportunities to travel and get away.

Pat Kronenberg was one of Joree's teachers in her high school years. Pat has spent seven years caring for Joree three or four afternoons per week in the evenings. Pat has a special relationship with Joree, having been with her many times at school and at home. She has a gentle and caring heart and has been so faithful over the years.

Rose Wilsey came into Joree's life in 2000, just two years after we arrived in Arizona. We know that Rose was sent from God. She immediately bonded with Joree and cares for her with the devotion and love of a mother. Rose spent countless hours in our home over the years, many of those without compensation. Rose is part of our family, and we have been blessed to have her travel with us or to stay in our home for weeks at a time so we could be away.

I know that if Joree could speak, she would tell everyone she knows how special Grandma Rose is. Grandma Rose is seventy-five years old. She still spends weekends with us and Joree. There are special crowns waiting for Rose in heaven. We could never say thank you enough to Rose for her commitment to our family. Joree will forever be blessed. Thank you, Rose.

People have said to us over the years, "I don't think I could do what you do; it is an amazing thing you do." While that is very kind, I usually answer that Joree has taught us much more than we have ever taught her. If you are a caregiver, parent, or just a friend of someone with special needs, you understand. If not, I would encourage anyone to consider volunteering, exploring a caregiver position, or looking into adoption. Jesus said what we do for the least of these touches his heart. I promise that you won't be disappointed with the time spent; ask Pat and Rose.